Forward

Freeriding has evolved rapidly. In the early days of my youth, every moment in the burgeoning sport was defining. In the gravel pits and clay hoodoos of Kamloops, British Columbia stood strong as a central fixture in the birth of this sport. It was here, in my hometown, where I—and many others like me—would find this path.

There was a major disconnect with what we were doing in the dusty interior of B.C. when compared to the rest of the mountain biking world. We had found a new way to have fun on two wheels, figuratively breaking fresh ground while literally riding new terrain (and breaking new bikes). Hucking off cliffs and building jumps in natural terrain was a unique approach to the sport, and some said we were the anarchists of mountain biking. Maybe they were right. The point was, in our corner of the world no one was telling us what we should or shouldn't ride, so we rode everything. It was liberating.

B.C. mountain bikers embraced freeriding early and rode hard with the concept; ride where you want, try new things, be free. Across the world, riders of all nationalities soon learned to manipulate terrain and use natural landscapes to do things on bikes that no one had ever imagined possible. The sport exploded and freeriding became the renegade answer to the question the bike industry was unknowingly asking itself all along:

"Where are we going?"

As one of the founders of freeriding, I am lucky to have been present for many of the defining moments of the sport. Documenting these moments has been my business, and mountain biking has been my life. After completing the New World Disorder series, Freeride Entertainment decided to quit at the height of our success. Year after year, this film series had chronicled the progression of freeriding, and hinted at what would come next. Now it was simply gone.

It felt like the end of the road. For a mountain biker, a more fitting analogy might be the end of the trail.

"**In the year following,** there was a lot of soul searching. During the process, the same question that brought freeriding out of the shadows and into the mainstream would arise again and again:

"Where are we going?"

In life, there are basic truths...answers to questions that never change. In freeriding, it is much the same. And the answer that was correct all those years ago is still right today.

The answer is "forward." We're moving forward, and we're doing it with the same sense of discovery and exploration as when we first pioneered those gravel pits so long ago."

One thing about the end of the trail is the knowledge that the ride is over. We want to change that. Because where this trail ends is just the beginning. Where the Trail Ends was made to inspire riders to go further. To be frightened. To find their way by getting lost first.

I know it helped me find my path. I hope it helps the sport I've loved for so long to do the same.

Thank You.

DEREK WESTERLUND
FOUNDER, FREERIDE ENTERTAINMENT

This book is a limited edition print:
_135_ OF 3,000

I've been working on this film for so long
I sometimes forget all the amazing
places I've been to.

" Behind every photo, there is always a story.
In the back alleys of Cafayate, Argentina,
Brad McgHegor and myself went on a mission
early one morning to find a home of plexiglass
that we could hide behind to take a huge
blast of recoil right to the ___ lens. Brad
wanted a big enough piece that we could hide
both of our cameras and if possible, our
bodies as well. On our hunt for the special glass
we ___ stumbled upon the perfect shop.
It was a basic shop and there was no way
they were going to have the modern plexiglass
that we were looking for, but it turned out
they had something even better, a perfectly
cut half inch thick piece of normal glass.
Normal glass is even better for this type of
shot because ___ scratch nearly as easily
and can be used ___ time. My only
question to Brad was ___ happen if it
break on us ___
half inch piece of ___ of us
as a rider came in ___ throwing
up rocks. "There is ___ breaking
look how thick it is! It was so stable,
he had found the ultimate tool for this shot
of the day!! It was all ___ she does not
aint seen its hardly ___ this piece of
glass on the side of that mountain for
Andrew and Serge to shoot we ___
they had...

"UNTIL VICTORY, ALWAYS" — ERNESTO GUEVARA

The following example gives some insight regarding the mountain land masses throughout the world. The land surface of the world covers approximately 91,730,100 square kilometers, of which 4,345,110 are above 3,000 meters. The Central Asian Highlands constitute the largest land mass over 3,000 meters, with close to 1,609,300 square kilometers above this height. South America has some 582,700 square kilometers. All the rest of the land above 3,000 meters is of little consequence on a world-wide basis.

OVER 90 PEAKS
OVER 22,966 FT.
EARTH'S HIGHEST AT 29,029.

WHERE THE TRAIL ENDS

Copyright© 2012 Red Bull Media House North America, Inc.

All photographs, interviews, artwork and text copyrights remain held by their respective authors / publishers.

First published in the United States of America in 2012 by Red Bull Media House North America, Inc.

Produced & Edited By Ben Bryan / Derek Westerlund / Joel Brinson.

This book documents the travels of, and would be impossible without, Freeride Entertainment.

Special Thanks to Scott Bradfield / Greg Jacobs / Patrice Radden / Werner Brell / Amy Detwiler.

The Impetus: Darren Berrecloth / Jeremy Grant

Principle Wordsmith: Mike Berard
Creative Direction: Joel Brinson
Photo Editor: Nicholas Schrunk
Primary Illustrator: Tyler Grobowsky
Additional Art & Design: Peter Line / Ryan Ilano
Print Coordination: Brian Campbell / Kurt Novak

All rights reserved. No part of this publication may be reproduced, stored in a retrieval system, or transmitted in any form or by electronic, mechanical, photocopying, or otherwise, without prior written consent of the publisher and copyright holders.

FIRST EDITION 2012
PRINTED IN THE USA BY LITHOGRAPHIX, INC.
BOUND BY ROSWELL
TYPE SET IN MERCURY / HOEFLER / GOTHAM
ISBN: 978-0-615-68432-1

[06.01.10 - 06.05.12]

The State of Freeriding

DEFINITION: PEOPLE OF THE MOUNTAINS

Utah: derived from the Colorado River Numic, also called Ute /'juːt/, Southern Paiute /'paɪjuːt/, and Ute-Southern Paiute or Southern Paiute-Ute.

Birthplace(s)

Roasting in the rain shadow of the Sierra Nevada mountain range, the arid mesas of Southern Utah were originally deemed inhospitable by white settlers, despite a long history of sedentary civilization by the Ute and Paiute peoples. Centuries later, mountain bikers who originally found their path in the pastoral green hills of Northern California's Marin County would travel over the Sierras as the rain could not and discover a different, harsher landscape to continue growing the roots of their sport.

People come to Utah to get lost. Or to be left alone. And whether that involves wholesale rejection of established norms or not, Utahans are characterized most by their fierce desire to be free. When mountain biking arrived, it rejected the old way of riding in the same fashion and broke open exactly what it meant to be a mountain biker.

The small outpost of Virgin fixates prominently in this Utahan legacy. As the location of the iconic Red Bull Rampage the town and its topography have contributed greatly to the shape of big mountain riding. It's here where Bender first made his mark in the red soil. It's here where Gracia first showed the two-wheeled world that racers could freeride. And it's here where Semenuk showed that world there are no limits, especially when you refuse them outright. This is where it all began, and where it will never end.

"Only the unknown frightens men.

But once a man has faced the unknown, that terror becomes the known." - Antoine de Saint-Exupery

MEASUREMENT CONVERSION FACTORS

Multiply	By	To Obtain
Millimeters	.03937	Inches
Centimeters	.3937	Inches
Centimeters	.03281	Feet
Meters	39.37	Inches
Meters	3.281	Feet
Meters	1.0936	Yards
Kilometers	.62137	Miles
Knots	1.1516	MPH

Right: today
Below: today

Slab—A relatively smooth portion of rock laying at an angle, usually 30° to 75° from the horizontal.

TRAINING CIRCULAR
NO. 90—6—1

hell-bent on self-destruction,

debris passive

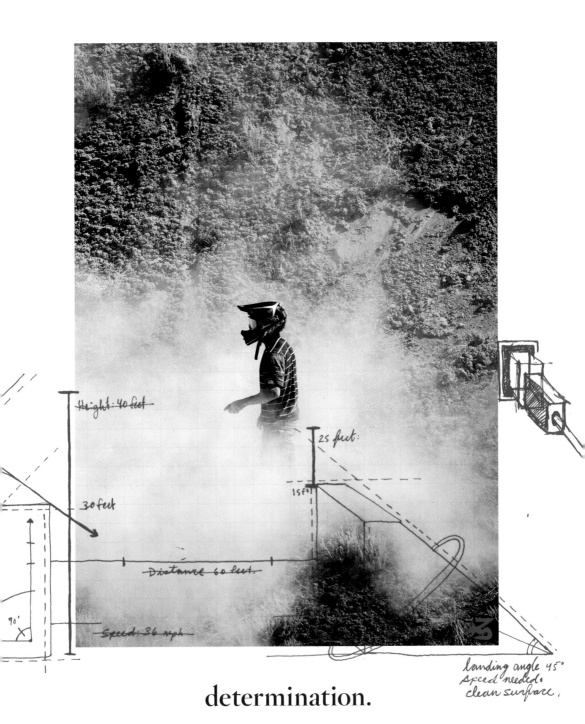

Height: 40 feet

25 feet:

30 feet

15 ft

Distance 60 feet

90°

Speed: 36 mph

23

landing angle 45°
speed needed.
clean surface.

determination.

1—2. Roads and Trails

Existing roads and trails offer the easiest routes in the mountains. Most follow valleys between ridges, crossing ridges and divides by passes.

HOLY LAND

UTAH.5:32 PM.LANDSCAPE.SHOT-58

The obsession of wanting something
new, will be replaced by the obsession

The sun sets on a mountain of potential.

FROM VIRGIN TO LEGEND

Utah's place in freeriding cannot be argued. This rugged piece of land has played an important hand in the development of the sport, and will continue to provide the proving grounds for future generations.

It is time to leave what we know so well.

Go off into the unknown.

We could ride Utah forever.

It will never get old, it will always be the best.

New places to ride here are ending.

The opportunities for us elsewhere are endless.

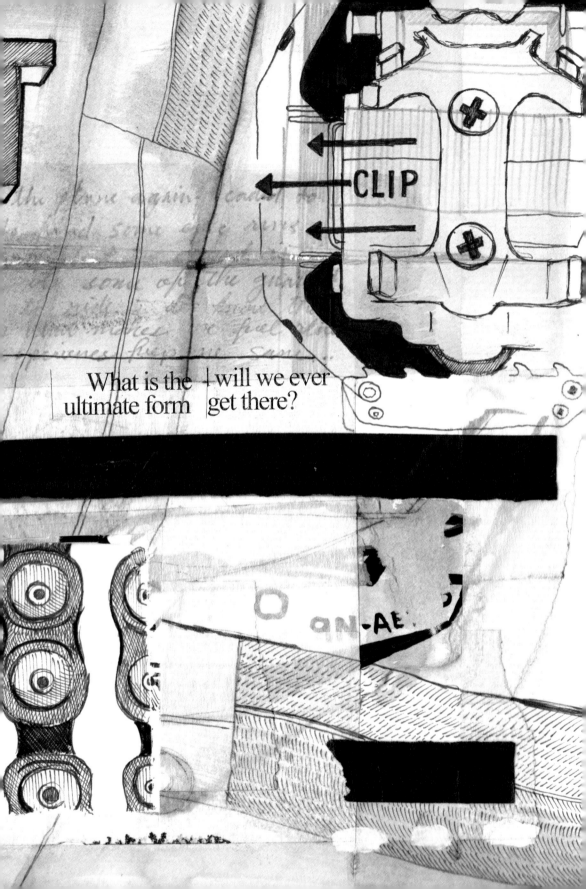

CLIP

What is the ultimate form | will we ever get there?

Gobi (001)

UNCERTAINTY

John Cage tells us that not knowing where to begin is a common form of paralysis. His advice: begin anywhere.

Unfamiliar Territory

THE SHIFTING SANDS OF THE GOBI DESERT MEET THE
UNCERTAINTY OF TRAVELING

A 1,295,000 square kilometer desert in northern China and southern Mongolia, the Gobi is one of the largest of its kind in the world. While the word "Gobi" means desert in Mongolian, what the desert means to modern explorers is much harder to define. The fossil fuel-rich region first became valuable to foreigners as the locale for several cities along the Great Silk Road. The trade route traveled through the powerful Mongol Empire, most famous for rulers Kublai Khan and Genghis Khan. The empire fell apart in 1396 AD, and parts of it were washed over by the sands of the Gobi.

Over 600 years later, Freeride returned to sample impressive fall lines that call to mind the big mountain ski and snowboard descents of Alaska and B.C.'s Coast Range. It's here where riders faced sandstorms and the threat of the Chinese Ministry of State Security to pioneer new routes on mountains that have never seen rubber knobs.

"Everyday we drove over an hour each way from our film locations," says Zink "China has crazy highways with insane passing. It's probably the reason foreigners aren't allowed to drive there. Well, that and the language barrier."

More than the language would challenge Zink, who required a hospital visit after crashing on the first run of the first day. "On the two hour drive to the hospital Zink winced in pain over every bump in the road." Says Freeride Entertainment cinematographer Cory Horton "I'll never forget the look on his face when the doctor told him nothing was broken. Zink took a few days off then laid down some of the sickest lines of the trip. He is one of the gnarliest people I know."

Despite China's bureaucratic and native obstacles, the Gobi's riches were as deep and endless as the shifting sands that make it up, reminding us all again of the fickle nature of struggle vs. reward.

APPROACHED FOR TWO DAYS,

COVERING TRACKS

"I set up to take a few shoots of the town we were staying in. Within seconds a traffic officer came over and put his hands over my lens. After a few minutes of futile communication, a number of other police arrived along with two plain-clothed guys from the military. You could tell immediately by the way they carried themselves that they were not just traffic cops. In almost perfect English, one of the Special Forces-looking guys asked us for our permits and passports.

We went back to our hotel to speak to our guides. After a few hours at the hotel and numerous visits from other military personal we were allowed to continue shooting but would have to allow the military to view the footage at the end of our trip. Afraid of having it confiscated, we made a number of copies and distributed them throughout our crew."

– Cory Horton

2—49 *Cliff evacuation—descent*

Descent.

Berrecloth corners inches from the edge of a cliff at least 100-feet tall.

James Doerfling roosts up the dust in the golden Gobi evening glow.

Once your tires have been in this soil, there is nothing like it.

Loose and fast 101 with James Doerfling.

Earn your turns

Blind run-in, diving board take-off. Nervous and unsure, James Doerfling ‍ed up and hit it anyway.

I think what's exci
compromised by co
you understan
the freer you are

ingredients

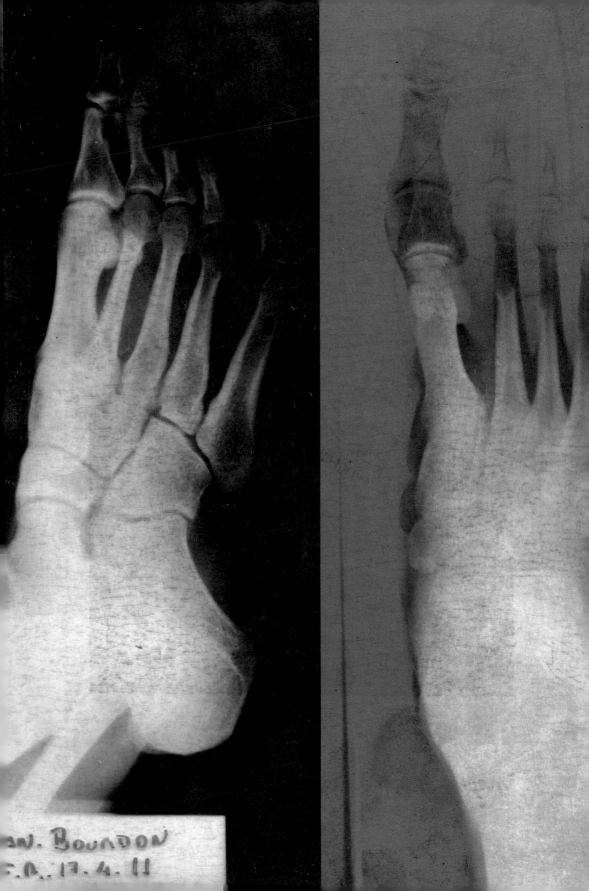
N. BOURDON
F.R. 17.4.11

James Doerfling roosts up the dust in the golden Gobi evening glow.

Once your tires have been in this soil, there is nothing like it.

Loose and fast 101 with James Doerfling.

BEFORE JAMES DROPPED THIS CLIFF HE SAYS TO ME "I DON'T KNOW ABOUT THIS MAN" IT WAS A BLIND RUN IN, LIKE A "DIVING BOARD" AS RIDERS SOMETIMES REFER TO IT AS I TOLD HIM IF HE WASN'T FEELING IT TO SAVE IT. HE HIKED UP AND DROPPED IN.

Blind run-in, diving board take-off. Nervous and unsure, James Doerfling ___ed up and hit it anyway.

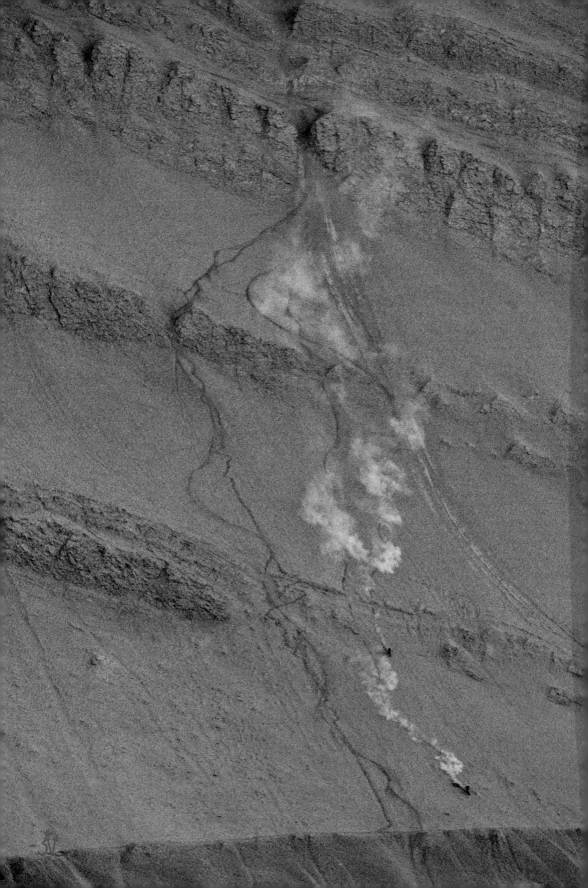

ingredients

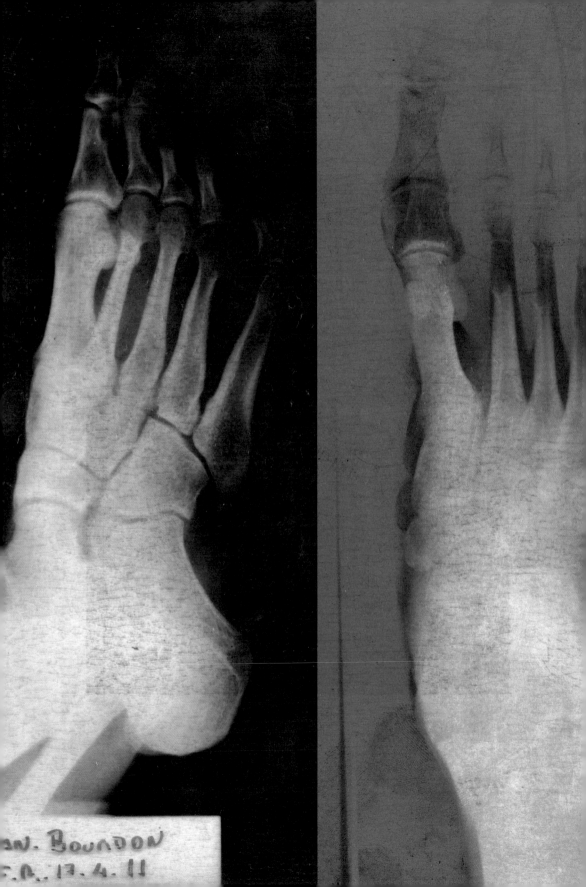

N. BOURDON

F.A. 17. 4. 11

Hard Times

"BETTER TO DIE STANDING THAN TO LIVE ON YOUR KNEES."

-ERNESTO 'CHE' GUEVARA

Going to the Gobi Desert was like being picked up and being transported to another planet. We jumped into a climate that gets 16mm of rain per YEAR and AVERAGES temperatures in summer of 40 degrees celsius. Nothing is familiar, everything is an adventure, from the markets where raw meat hangs in the heat ready to be bought and eaten to the beds, which are harder than sleeping on cement. The sounds, the smells, the heat and the near misses in traffic everyday on the road keep us remembering that we are far, far from home. A fellow traveler once told me, "in these countries ones heart is never at rest."

Argentina

Beneath it all, Argentina goes above and beyond expectations
Red wine and meat. Friendly locals. Bureaucracy and pride.
Argentina challenged us and we rose to the occasion, coming
away for a newfound appreciation for the land of contrast.

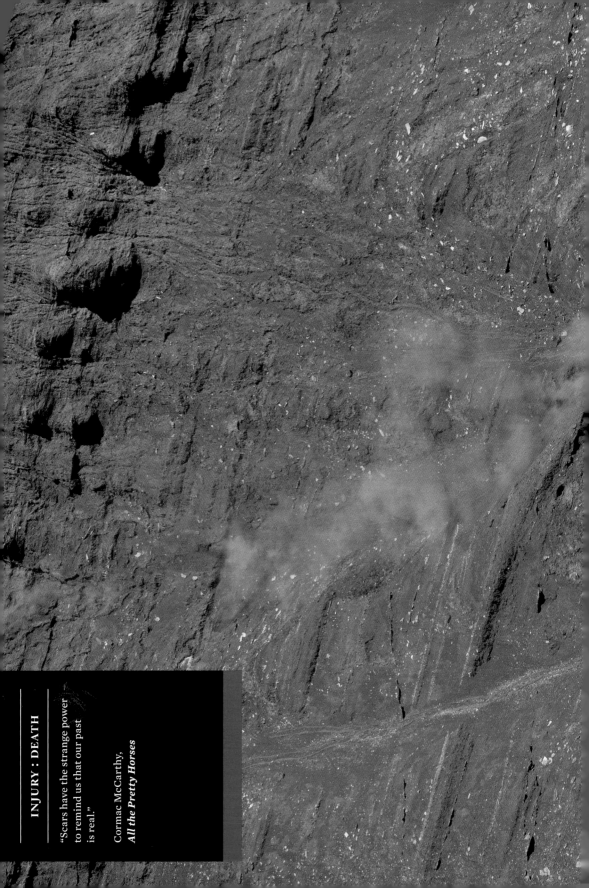

INJURY : DEATH

"Scars have the strange power
to remind us that our past
is real."

Cormac McCarthy,
All the Pretty Horses

Argentine Shutdown
LOGGING FOOTAGE IN S. AMERICA

"Robbie Bourdon and I were shooting up a long drainage off the main road while the other crews were working a few ridges over. I had clear view of the valley floor and our rental vans. I noticed a dirt bike coming up the wash and—worried about someone stealing our camera gear or bikes—I radioed the other crew to warn them. Jeremy [Grant] went down to talk to them. After a few minutes of discussion, Jeremy instructed us to stay on the ridges and hide the tools and camera gear. The rider had been a park ranger, and we were in a restricted area.

We went back to the hotel and for a day or two and waited to hear if we were allowed to carry on shooting. I remember feeling like we had all worked so hard to get here and stay here and it could all be for nothing."

– Cory Horton, cinematographer

Barrocloth Descent / Frame 2
ARGENTINA. 4:56 PM. DIGI.SHOT 47

Berrecloth Descent / Frame 3
ARGENTINA.4:32 PM.DIGI.SHOT-11

Whip #302A

ARG.1:21 PM.SHOT-80867

Allow yourself to wander aimlessly. Explore adja-
cencies. Lack judgment. Be

Boost II / Mobbing

ARG. 4:39 PM. SHOT-60065

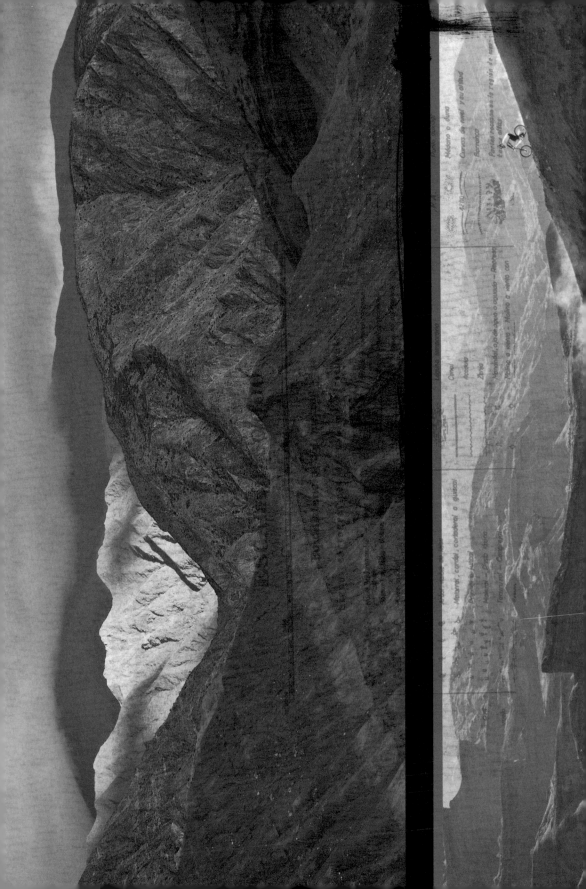

sheer labor and force of will.

experience
process as a struggle   drop,

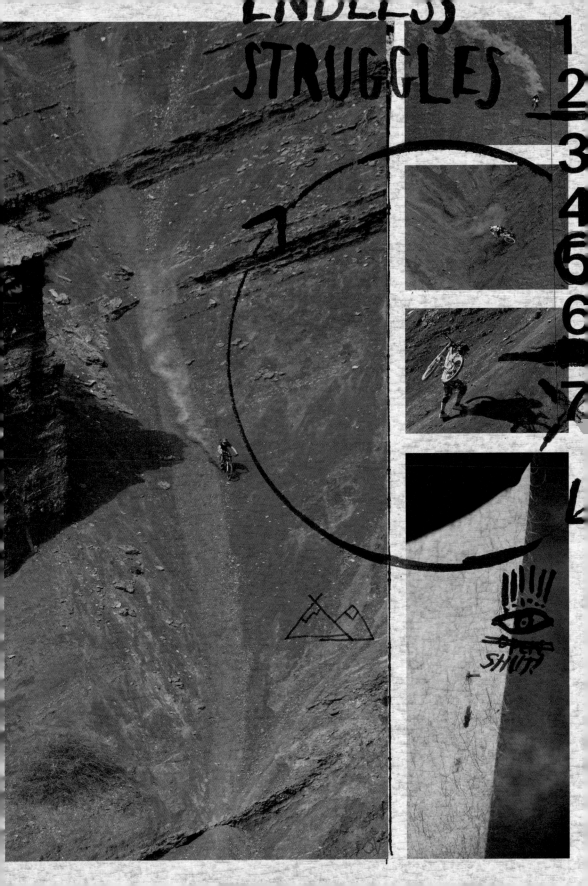

STORIED
ARCS

"One of the doorways presents a vision.!"

Fraser River

BRITISH COLUMBIA

3. There is an ideal
   I would even say madness that
   can exist
   with all the freedom that is to be
   found

"I should consider the passage down to be certain death in nine attempts out of ten. I shall therefore no longer talk about it as a navigable stream."
– Simon Fraser

ALTERNATIVE TRANSPORT

"Having shot mountain biking in B.C. for more than 15 years, I remember feeling like the Fraser River was going to be an easy shoot. It wasn't.

The 10-square kilometer zone we chose to shoot in was only accessible by jet boat and helicopter. Each day the crew and riders would have to walk from where the boat dropped us off into the zone. Carrying all the gear you needed for the day. This was OK for the first few days but then became a mission by the end of the week—as people became tired and sore, the trek became longer. Thank God we had amazing camp support with unbelievable food. Even though I walked everyday I'm sure I gained weight from all the food."

– Cory Horton

There are mountains in virtually every country in the world and because of this, almost every war that has been fought since the start of recorded history has included some type of mountain operations. It can be assumed that this pattern will not change and troops will again be fighting in mountainous terrain in any future war.

Basic tactics for mountain operations have not changed. What has changed is the equipment and means of transport. The helicopter gives almost immediate access to terrain which in former times was completely out of reach, or could be reached only after hours of tedious climbing. This fact holds true only as long as good weather exists. ~~If the weather turns bad,~~

Backyard Flow

BRITISH COLUMBIA'S MIGHTY FRASER RIVER BEARS WITNESS TO
MODERN EXPLORATION

Some things can be right under your nose your entire life and you may never find them.

The same goes for places. Growing up in a mountain biking town in B.C., I know we have some of the best terrain in Canada—maybe the world—for riding, but we can only access what the roads and trails will allow us to. That is, unless you factor in the rivers.

The Cariboo Chilcotin Coast is home to over 10,000 km of rivers. At one time, explorers used river ways like these to find new routes over strange lands. It was time to get on the rivers and go back in time, in order to push the sport of mountain biking into the future.

When Freeride Entertainment launched the idea to navigate the longest river in British Columbia over a two-week period, camping and searching for new land to ride, my first thoughts were that we would be exploring the land just like the early explorer Simon Fraser did. In his discovery of the river, Fraser found a trade passage to the Pacific Ocean. We would have a different agenda and a different set of tools; a 20-person, flat-hulled, aluminum, twin V8 engine jet boat and nine-inch travel bicycles. Our mountain bikes were about to go places that most people may never even see on a map, let alone in person.

The captain for the journey would be my good friend and local legend of the river, Doug Green. Green had traveled the world, eventually settling on the banks of the Fraser where he grew up. He bought the biggest, most badass boat he could find, and has since been making a living off his passions; exploring and story telling.

After an enormous first day navigating the river and setting up camp, we realized we'd neglected to account for bearproofing our vast reserves of food. For the next 10 days, one person would stand guard over the food, armed and ready for any visitors from the bears that call this land home, so far away from the human footprint.

B.C. still retains the hidden treasures explorers first came for 200 years ago.

exploration is vast in scope

Derek Westerlund on Douglas Green
FRASER RIVER, BRITISH COLUMBIA

Fraser River would not have been possible without team work. Douglas Green of Caribou Chilcotin JetBoat Adventures was instrumental in making this possible. His knowledge of the rivers was unsurpassed. We truly could not have been with a better person. He was a role model for respecting this environment and riding where wildlife and the river rule. He educated the crew on how to pull off a trip like this. Dustin Lindgren, who spearheaded the trip, has guided and shot most of the world's great rivers.

HOME AWAY FROM HOME

You have many cultural experiences in your lifetime. Some will never be forgotten.
Camping rituals remain the same no matter what culture you come from.

A campfire, six strings and 14 cases of beer. Friendships that last a lifetime.

1. ....Hydration first
2. ....Lining up for dinner
3. ....The storied Fraser River sturgeon
4. .... Stimulation strumming
5. ....They only come out at night
6. ....Bear bait never tasted so good
7. ....Basecamp
8. ....Fubar
9. ....Cory Horton and Sorge knuckle up

MOUNTAIN
HEAD

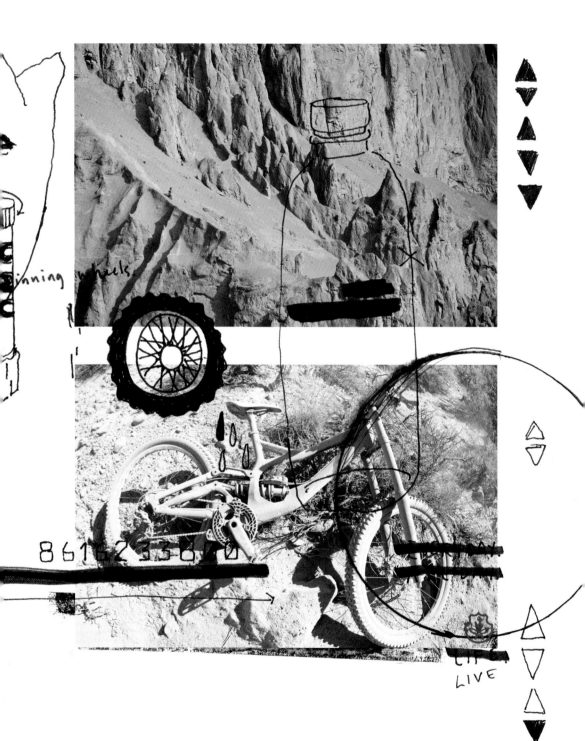

inning wheels

86162338?0

LIVE

The Gateway Drug

THE ALLURE OF NEPAL'S UNIQUE LANDSCAPE PULLS LIKE GRAVITY

Crazy story. The plane that we shot in this shot actually went down. Blaker, Myself & Nick were all supposed to be on the returning flight that went down.

Important Notice

1. Aliens who do not lodge at hotels, guesthouses or inns shall, within 24 hours (72 hours in rural areas) of entry, go through accommodation registration at local police station.

2. Aliens holding visas Z, X or J-1 shall, within 30 days of entry, apply for Residence Permits to the exit-entry department of the public security bureau of the city where the applicants reside.

3. Aliens shall not be employed in China without permission of the competent authorities of the Chinese Government.

4. Aliens who reside or stay in China shall carry with themselves their passports or Residence Permits for possible examination.

5. In case of emergency, please dial 110 to seek help from police.

postponement in the schedule

Riding Nepal

THE KINGDOM OF MUSTANG AND THE WINDS OF CHANGE

Vancouver to Hong Kong to Bangkok to Kathmandu. A private flight to Jomsom. A high-mountain highway voyage followed by a three-day mule train moving a literal ton of gear. At 15,000 feet, the air is thin. Above us, the 8168-meter peak of Dhaulagiri stands slightly higher than the famous 8091-meter Annapurna 1. Vertical cliffs house inaccessible caves where people inexplicably lived 2000 years ago. The landscape is a barren moonscape of eroded sandstone pillars. Untouched by modern civilization, life in Mustang goes on as it has for centuries in unhurried pace. We must move at this pace, not only because we're forced to, but because this mysterious and culture-rich land deserves it.

Here, the influence of the outside world—and especially China—is growing. One of the few regions where we could escape foreigners like ourselves, Mustang, Nepal was only recently opened to the world. The forbidden Kingdom was opened to the outside world in March of 1992. We arrive less than 20 years later to this "fertile plain" (translated from the Tibetan name mun tan), in search of our own fertile grounds. However we have no plans for the plains. We come for the mountains.

Things move differently here. When we first arrive in Kathmandu, every one of our 50-plus pieces of luggage miraculously arrives, except for Zink's bike. Five days later, his bike appears on the doorstep of a teahouse. When the tractor hired to deliver the bike broke down coming up a deep river valley, a porter walked the rest of the journey with the bike hanging off a forehead strap. A grateful Zink enjoyed "some of the most amazing riding of my life" due to the hard work of that porter.

Every day, the wind would arrive on schedule. Between 9 and 10 am the gusts would roar up the valleys, shutting down the shoot. Early mornings. Frozen nights. Eight-hour drives through narrow canyons and over pockmarked roads in military vehicles. One day, we hike 20 miles through mountainous terrain.

On the final day, our second flight out is sidelined due to the ever-present wind. Three of the crew make the decision to make a midnight drive out. The next day the flight they were scheduled to be on goes down in the mountains, reminding us all the dangers that come with curiosity.

Nepal was one of the hardest and most rewarding trips of our lives.

The characteristic contrails of Nepal follow the rubber stamp of tire on soil. Here the bicycle's path is lit by more than the impact—it is ethereal.

COMMUNITY.

NEPALESE TOWN #76E

Back when the game started 15 years ago, freeride specific bikes were non-existent. Warmed over downhill bikes were the weapon of choice. Of course, freeride was not DH, so bars broke. Rear triangles contorted. Crank arms bent and twisted on the smallest of cliff drops. As riders pushed their limitations, technology followed. No longer were riders talking grams. They were talking tensile strength. They wanted bikes that could take the brute force of frequent crashes in rugged terrain. Every year, the manufacturers caught up with stronger equipment, and then the riders would break it, forcing the industry to keep pace. This cyclical relationship carries on to this day, allowing both bike and rider to push a little further each year, in the name of progress.

WE TRIED TO PLAN AHEAD FOR WIND AND DUST WE'D ENCOUNTER ON THE TRIP OUT, KNOWING IT WOULD BE A SANDSTORM IN THE BACK OF THE TRUCK. JEREMY HAD BOUGHT A LITTLE PIECE OF CHEETAH PRINT CLOTH. ONCE THE DUST STARTED TO FLY THE BANDANAS WENT UP AND THE SHADES WENT ON. WE STARTED ARGUING ABOUT WHICH SIDE OF THE TRUCK WAS MORE COMFORTABLE AND THAT'S WHEN ZINK HIT US WITH "LOOK AT YOU GUYS! CHEETAHFACE AND THE SUNGLASSES!" THE NAME STUCK – OUR FEARLESS LEADER, CHEETAHFACE, LEADING US OUT OF NEPAL LIKE A GROUP OF REBELS TAKING OVER A REGIME.

FutureSt
SUSPENSION THAT WO

मून

REMOTE MONASTERY #41F

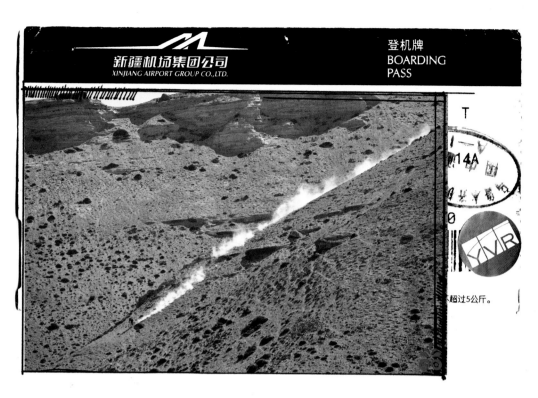

超过5公斤。

you're fifth gear pinned, I'm eighth gear pinned buddy!

1 Kathmandu Valley 1:50000	5 Shorong/Hinku 1:50000	9 Annapurna 1:100000
2 Khumbu Himal 1:50000	6 Tamba Kosi 1:50000	21 Kathmandu City 1:10000
3 Lapchi Kang 1:50000	7 Dudh Kosi 1:50000	22 Patan City 1:7500
4 Rolwaling Himal 1:50000	8 Helambu-Langtang 1:100000	

I really fell in love with the

95

I really fell in love with the people
in Nepal. The woman in this shot was
suffering from a abscessed tooth and
the nearest dentist was a 10 day walk,
yet she was still smiling.

This is me smiling at the summit of the biggest hike/bike day of my life.

| 4000 | 13123 | 6200 | 20341 | 8400 | 27559 | Kartographische Anstalt **Freytag-Berndt** |

495   87°00' | 500

You just had to have the energy to get out there

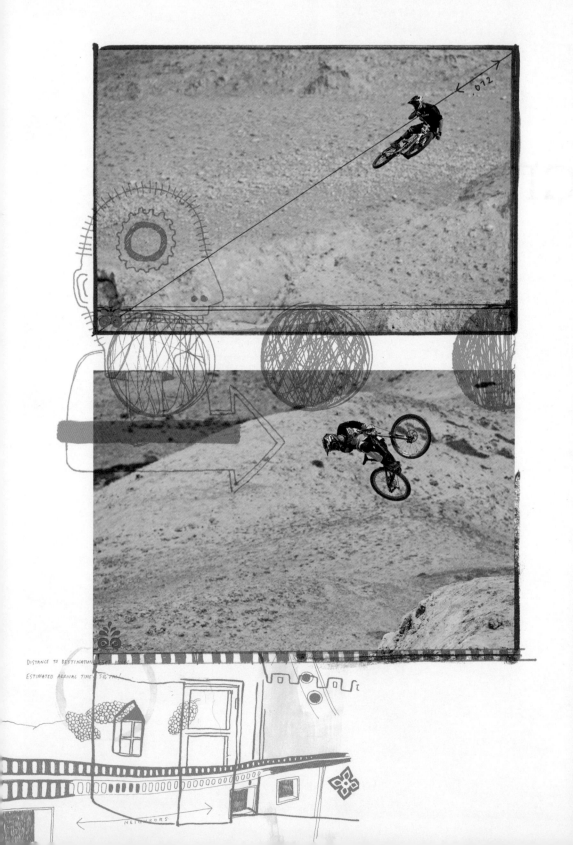

那拉提 大气磅礴的西部风光
The magnificent western prospect of the Nalati

http://

咨询电话: 0999-5291888   Consulting Tel·0999-5291888

CLASSIC CREST

he found photographs to perfection

- The Making of

Editing doesn't wait for the studio. A momentary desk is as good a place as any to log footage.

RUPEES ONE HUNDRED

文提旅游风景区
://www.nalati.com/

"MANY CALL ME AN ADVENTURER AND THAT I AM,
ONLY ONE OF A DIFFERENT SORT: ONE OF THOSE
WHO RISKS HIS SKIN TO PROVE HIS PLATITUDES."

-ERNESTO 'CHE' GUEVARA

Watching chinese kids ride a dh bike for
the first time was insane. These kids
just grabbed our bikes and started
shredding.

crazy story! The you

evasses and ice

sion

656 ft
131 ft
in metres

Contours

Conversio

m
4600
4800
5000
5200
5400
5600
5800
6000
6200
6400
6600

KISS OF THE KHUKRI

ur intervals at d

30°   20°

"On day 16, we tried to squeeze one last day of shooting in. Our guides told us that we could cut a day off the trip back to Jomsom if we hired a cargo truck to take us through the dried up riverbed. This sounded good...until we saw the river wasn't dry, the truck wasn't comfortable, and it'd be a 12-hour trip.

The drive was rough as hell. The river occasionally submerged the bed of the truck with water. Zink and Sorge had to hang off the tailgate to balance us out. At one point, we passed a gorge so steep we all jumped off in fear, except McGregor and our medic, who road on top of the truck all the way down to the riverbed.

We passed the time drinking Khukri Rum and singing. We left at 6:30AM and arrived to a sunset at 8:45PM. It was an epic end to an epic trip."

– Nicholas Schrunk, cinematographer

life, absurdity, and the world around us

Where does the border lie

approach,
embrace

Where The Wild Things Were

I CARRIED THE EPIC
CAMERA TO KEEPER
SAFE. I COULDN'T
BELIEVE THE
PORTERS IN NEPAL
THEY'RE THE
STRONGEST GUYS
I'VE EVER SEEN.
ONE GUY CARRIED
A 60 POUND STEADICAM
BOX ON HIS
BACK AND HEAD
FOR 12 HOURS
THROUGH THE MOUNTAINS
SMILING THE WHOLE TIME

The Return to Zion

THE PARTY LINE!

with stylistic uniformity, each character rendered in the same vein and
aimed at creating a more 'seamless' experience

BLASTER

SO
SUBTRACT
SO

AFTER US, WHAT REMAINS ???
WHAT HAVE WE LEFT?
WHO WILL KNOW WE WERE EVER HERE?

FLIGHT INTERRUPTED

REDEMPTION

Utah : #213Z

#236C (New Ground)

Initiate sequence #026A

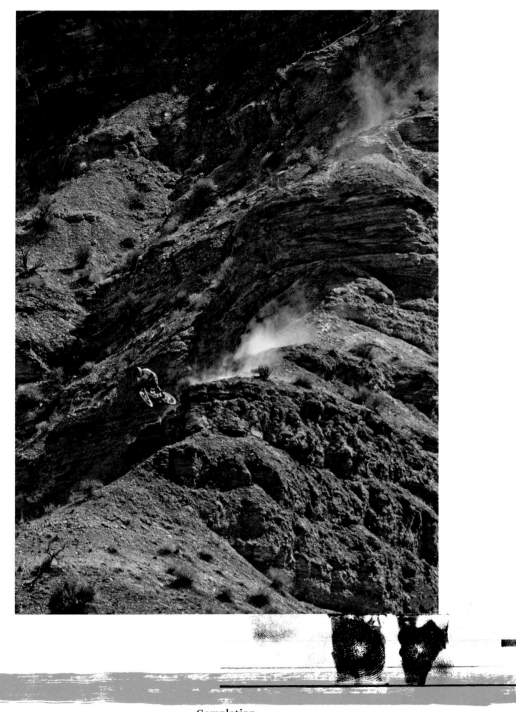

Completion.

à l'origine de frustrations,
frustration, endless debate

In the beginning

So where do we push ourselves next?

And how fast?

What is the outer limit of our potential?

And why does it matter?

The questions asked are the same ones man has asked since the dawn of consciousness. And they will continue to ask them. But the only way we will find the answer is to continue asking, and to continue riding beyond where the trail ends.

Where The Trail Ends: The Crew

WITHOUT THE SPONTANEOUS CREATIVITY OF THESE PEOPLE, THIS FILM WOULD NOT BE THE SAME.

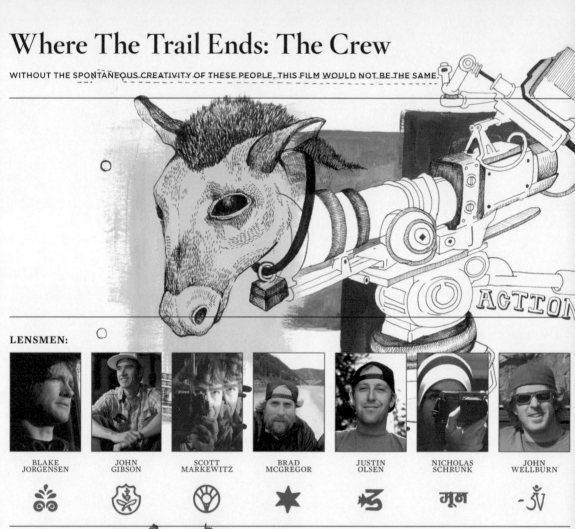

LENSMEN:

| BLAKE JORGENSEN | JOHN GIBSON | SCOTT MARKEWITZ | BRAD MCGREGOR | JUSTIN OLSEN | NICHOLAS SCHRUNK | JOHN WELLBURN |

Where The Trail Ends: The Riders

THE RIDERS LEADING AN ENDLESS EXPLORATION.

CAMERON ZINK

DARREN BERRECLOTH

KURTIS SORGE

JAMES DOERFLING

ANDREU LACONDEGUY

ROBBIE BOURDON

CAMERON McCAUL

TYLER McCAUL

GARETT BUEHLER

MIKE KINRADE

PAUL BASAGOITIA

Return to Gobi

"WHAT MAKES THE DESERT BEAUTIFUL IS
THAT IT HIDES, SOMEWHERE, A WELL."
- ANTOINE DE SAINT EXUPÉRY

— . This was my life for 2years, travelling, hiking, biking, camping & never being home!

I have been looking ████████ for years

MILEAGE: 5914 MILES
GOLD   /STAR GOLD
FLIGHT:UA   889Y

GATE: **94** SEAT:51C
DEPART: 109P
  SAN FRANCISCO
ARRIVE: 425P
  BEIJING
BOARD TIME: 1219P

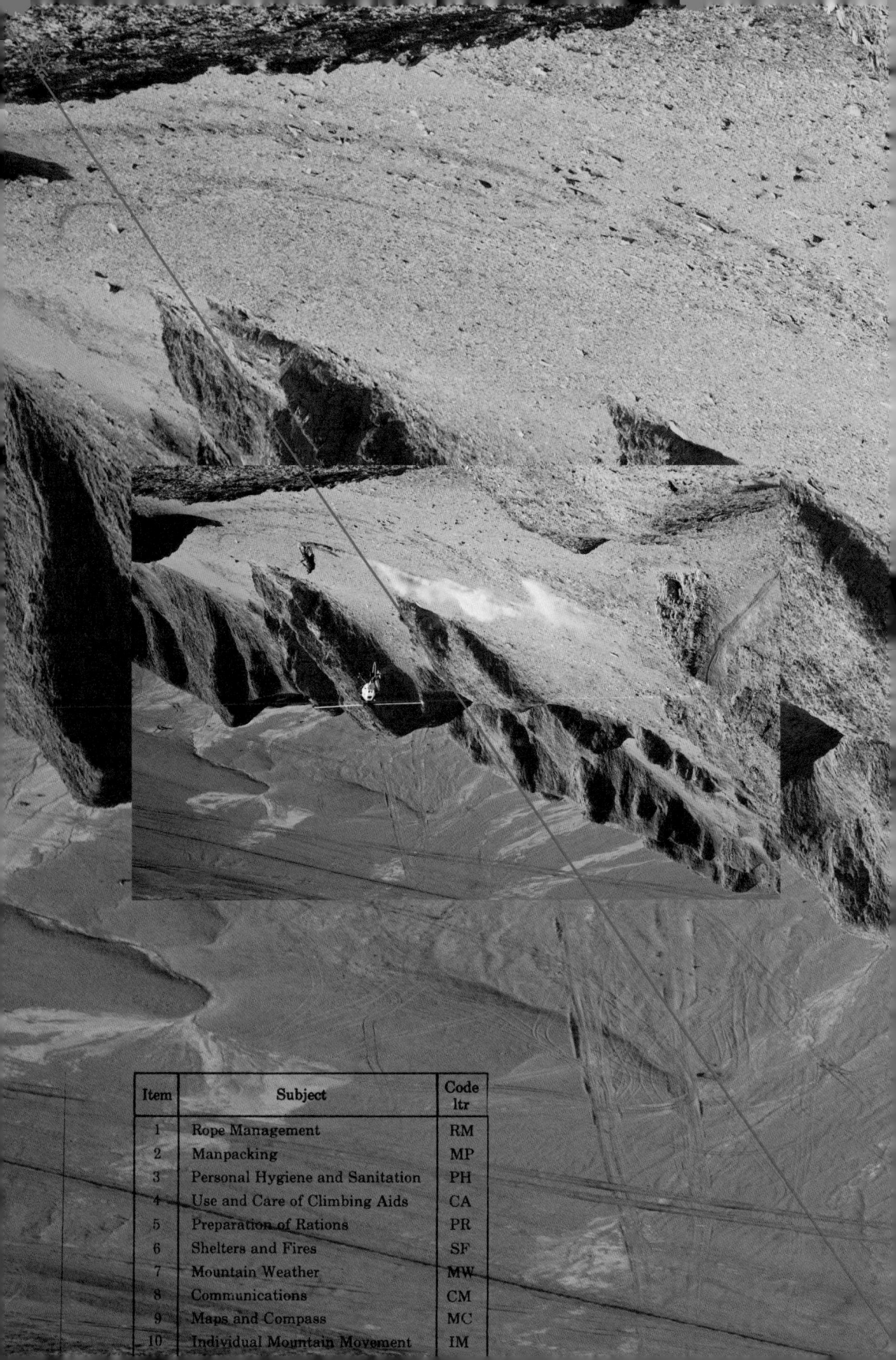

Item	Subject	Code ltr
1	Rope Management	RM
2	Manpacking	MP
3	Personal Hygiene and Sanitation	PH
4	Use and Care of Climbing Aids	CA
5	Preparation of Rations	PR
6	Shelters and Fires	SF
7	Mountain Weather	MW
8	Communications	CM
9	Maps and Compass	MC
10	Individual Mountain Movement	IM

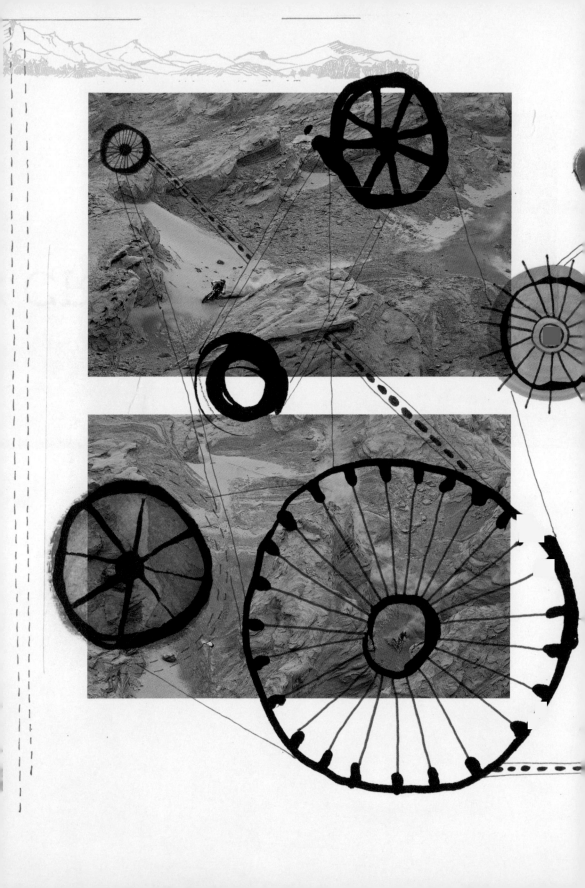

Skills kill

Behavioral Effects. Listed below are some of the behavioral effects that will be encountered in unacclimatized personnel:

- Increased errors in performing simple mental arithmetic.
- Decreased ability for sustained concentration.
- Deterioration of memory.
- Decreased vigilance.
- Increased irritability in some individuals.
- Impairment of night vision and some constriction in peripheral vision.

Self-evaluation is impaired in the same manner as if the person was intoxicated. During the first few days at high altitude, leaders will have extreme difficulty in maintaining a coordinated, operational unit. The roughness of the terrain and the harshness and variability of the weather add greatly to the difficulties of unacclimatized personnel. Although strong motivation may succeed in overcoming some of the physical handicaps imposed by the environment, the total impact will still result in errors of judgement by individual soldiers and officers alike.

the vantage point

2—49 Cliff evacuation—descent

Allow events to change you.